(25) Mini Math Mysteries

by Bill Johnson

SCHOLASTIC
PROFESSIONAL BOOKS

New York ❖ Toronto ❖ London ❖ Auckland ❖ Sydney

Cover design by Jaime Lucero

Cover illustration by Julie Durrell

Interior design by Ellen Matlach Hassell
for Boultinghouse & Boultinghouse, Inc.

Interior illustration by Teresa Anderko and Manuel Rivera

ISBN 0-590-76247-8

CONTENTS

INTRODUCTION

Math can intrigue children, surprise them, and excite them. Would they believe that they can have $1.19 in coins but not be able to make change for a dollar? Or that if their allowance is raised 10 percent this month and 10 percent next month, they'll get more than with a 30 percent raise next month?

The mysteries in this book are designed to arouse children's curiosity by presenting math problems in fresh and stimulating settings. Some of the stories will appeal to students because they relate to their everyday lives. Others rely on children's love of the wild and the wacky—from talking animals to trips in outer space.

The fun and excitement of these mysteries will capture children's attention and motivate them to do the math to arrive at the solution. Another thing that makes the problems so appealing is their focus on the process of solving a problem, rather than on the solution itself. Each question and answer section takes students through the problem-solving process, letting them see that there's no magic involved, but rather steps and strategies that they can master. So, if fun is the hook that draws them in, confidence is the power that keeps them going. In fact, each mystery asks students to do just that—keep on going—with a related problem. (In cases where there isn't enough space for that reinforcement on the question page, suggestions can be found in the Teacher Notes section of the answer key.)

Children also gain confidence in math by confronting the unexpected and finding out that it's not at all as frightening as it may appear. One mystery has children compare the areas of circles without needing to know the formula for finding such areas. Other mysteries enable children to confront very large numbers and complex fractions as easily as small and simple ones, so that they can see that what look like gorillas are really pussycats.

Choosing and Using the Mysteries

The mysteries help children develop a wide range of essential skills that are based on the NCTM Standards. Specific skills are highlighted in the Skills Box at the beginning of each mystery. With two exceptions, the mysteries are arranged in approximate order of difficulty. (The exceptions are Mystery 1, a trick that could serve as a warm-up, and Mystery 25, a clutch of mini-mysteries that could be used as a grand finale.) The sequence is intended simply as a guide; you can present the mysteries in any order.

Except for the "finale," each mystery has a story on the first page and fill-in questions, including more difficult Super-Challenges, on the second page.

The format is meant to be simple and flexible, so that you can adapt it to suit your needs and the needs of individual students. Presentation options include:

- ♣ duplicating both pages for children to read and answer individually or in groups
- ♣ duplicating just the story page and working through the questions orally with the class
- ♣ duplicating just the questions page and reading the story to the class
- ♣ reading the story page and working through the questions with the class
- ♣ duplicating and reading either the story, or the questions, or both

Suggestions for specific approaches and extensions in the Teacher Notes are meant to be just that—suggestions.

Necessary Materials

Students should have paper and pencil on hand to solve all the mysteries. If calculators are available, children may use them if you wish. (However, calculators aren't necessary for any of the computations.) A handful of mysteries require a few additional materials, such as cardboard and scissors; these are indicated in the Teacher Notes section.

Tips for Student Problem Solvers

When students get stuck on a problem, encourage them to ask themselves these key questions and to follow these guidelines:

* What am I supposed to do? What exactly is wanted? (Make sure I understand the problem.)

* What facts are given? Are they all necessary? Are they all in the simplest terms? (If necessary, I can jot down the key facts as briefly as possible. Sometimes a rough sketch will help.)

* Where is the logical place to begin?

* Does this problem resemble any others? (I can check to see if it's a kind of problem I've seen before. If so, I can tackle it the same way.)

* Is it a new kind of problem? (I can begin by trying *something*. The more problems I tackle, the more I'll learn how to cope with new problems. That's what these mysteries are all about!)

A Tricky Walk

This kind of puzzle has been getting wrong answers for hundreds of years. See if you can get it right!

"You'll never believe what I saw at 5:00 this morning!" Carmen said to her friend Pat. "I was riding my bike to Townsville to deliver papers. I was all alone, when suddenly I saw this strange parade coming toward me.

"It was the circus coming to town. First, there were three elephants, with two men riding on each of them. Then there were four big white horses, and they each had two women riders. Last of all, there were two open trucks. One had three clowns juggling balls. The other had three more clowns doing handstands and cartwheels. You should have seen them!

"Anyway, here's a question for you. How many people in all were on their way to Townsville at 5:00 this morning?"

"Wait a minute!" said Pat. "I can't remember everything you told me!"

Can you? How many people were there? _____

Name _Weston_   5-23-01

A Tricky Walk

Is 20 your answer? If so, you got some good calculation practice. But you didn't get the right answer!

The question asks how many were going **to** Townsville. The circus people were coming **from** Townsville. Only Carmen was going to Townsville. So the correct answer is 1.

Yes, that's a tricky question, but it points out that you need to read carefully. Some problems, like the mysteries in this book, have extra facts that don't help you answer the questions.

But in the **questions**, every fact matters. Try these.

1. **a.** Angie and Sue had $3.00 to spend. Angie bought a magazine for $1.25. Sue bought some candy for $0.50. How much did they have left? _$1.25_

    b. Angie and Sue each had $3.00 to spend. Angie bought a magazine for $1.25. Sue bought some candy for $0.50. How much did they have left? _$1.75   - $2.50_

2. **a.** Did you spot the extra word? What is it? _each_

    b. What is the difference between the amount they had left in **1a** and the amount they had left in **1b**? _$.50_

3. Greg was standing on Main Street. He asked the way to the library. He was told to walk north two blocks, then right two blocks, then left two blocks.

    a. Draw an X where he should have ended up.

    b. But Greg did not follow the directions carefully. He walked north two blocks, then left two blocks, then right two blocks. Draw a circle where he ended up.

    c. What mistake did Greg make? _left instead of right_

    _____

    d. How many blocks from the library did he end up? _Two_

How Many Cookies?

Karen and five friends were sitting in the kitchen when her Aunt Margo walked in. She pointed to a large plate on the counter.

"Well!" she said. "I left an odd number of cookies on that plate. Now it's turned into a different odd number. Isn't that odd?"

There were three cookies left.

"It's my birthday, so we ate some," said Karen. "Is that odd?"

"No," said Aunt Margo. "But the number was important. It's my birthday tomorrow. The number of cookies showed your age today and my age tomorrow."

"How could it do that?" said Karen. "You're several times older than I am."

"You'll see," said Aunt Margo. "Did anyone notice how many cookies there were?"

The children all shook their heads no.

"Then let's work it out," said Aunt Margo. "How many cookies did you each have?"

Karen had 3. Maria, Lester, and Nikki each had 4. Kevin had 5. But Liza wasn't sure if she had 3 or 4.

"We'll never work it out," Karen sighed.

"Sure you will," said Aunt Margo. "Just do a bit of odding—I mean *adding*—and you'll have the answer in a flash!"

Can you help them?

How Many Cookies?

1. There were 3 cookies left. Five of the children knew exactly how many cookies they ate.

   a. Start by adding those six numbers.

   $$3 + 3 + 4 + 4 + 4 + 5 = \underline{22}$$

   b. Liza didn't know if she ate 3 or 4 cookies. Suppose she ate 3. Add that to the total in **1a**:

   $$\underline{22} + 3 = \underline{25}$$

   c. Now suppose she ate 4 and add that to the total in **1a**:

   $$\underline{22} + 4 = \underline{26}$$

   d. Aunt Margo said she put an *odd* number of cookies on the plate.

   So the correct answer is _____25_____.

2. Then Aunt Margo explained that the answer was her age tomorrow. But the digits added up to Karen's age today. (In the number 48, the digits are 4 and 8.)

   a. How old was Karen? _____6_____

   b. Aunt Margo was several times older than Karen. How many times older? Keep multiplying Karen's age until you find the answer:

   $$\underline{6} \times 2 = \underline{12}$$

   $$\underline{6} \times 3 = \underline{18}$$

   $$\underline{6} \times 4 = \underline{24}$$

   $$\underline{6} \times 5 = \underline{30}$$

   c. So Aunt Margo was _____4_____ times older than Karen.

Mean Dream Butterflies

"I had a really weird dream last night," Bob said to his friend Milt. "Five giant butterflies landed right in front of me. Boy, did they look mean!"

"How can a butterfly look mean?" asked Milt.

Bob made a mean face. "That's how. Anyway, they talked mean, too. They said I couldn't wake up until I told them how many legs they had all together. Then they started dancing about so I couldn't count their legs."

"You didn't have to. Insects have 6 legs."

"I knew that! I multiplied 6 by 5 and told them the number. *'Wrong!'* they yelled. *'We're dream butterflies. We can have as many legs as we like. We could have zillions of legs or zero legs!'*"

"Zero legs would be easy to work out," said Milt.

"It wasn't easy," said Bob. "They yelled, *'Two of us have five legs each and the others have seven legs each. Try again, or we still won't let you wake up!'*"

"Did you try again?"

"I'm here, aren't I?"

How did Bob escape from the mean dream butterflies?

25 Mini Math Mysteries Scholastic Professional Books

Name _____

Mean Dream Butterflies

1. To warm up for this mystery, find Bob's first answer.

How many legs would five real butterflies have?   **5 x 6 =** _____

2. Now back to the dream butterflies.

   a. Milt said it would be easy if they each had zero legs.
   How many legs would the 5 butterflies have then? _____

   b. But they didn't have zero legs. How many of them had 5 legs? _____

   c. How many legs did those butterflies have in all? _____ **x 5 =** _____

   d. How many of the dream butterflies had 7 legs? _____

   e. How many legs did those have in all? _____ **x 7 =** _____

   f. So the total number of legs was _____ **+** _____ **=** _____.

That's not the end of the story. . . . .

3. SUPER-CHALLENGE! The next night, Bob dreamed
he was trapped between two huge swarms of butterflies.
The chief butterfly told him there were 1,000 butterflies
in front and another 1,000 in back. Those in front
had 5 legs each. Those in back had 7 legs each.
So there were more butterfly legs in back
of Bob than in front. How many more?
Bob had to answer quickly. . . .

Quickly, what's the answer?

_____

Hot and Cold

It was summer. Lee and his family were visiting friends in Canada. The sun was hot, and they were sitting in the shade.

Lee's radio reported the weather. "It's 25 degrees," said the announcer.

Lee sat up. "It can't be 25 degrees! We'd all be freezing."

"They're different degrees," said Maggie, his older sister. "We use the Fahrenheit scale. Canadians use the Celsius scale."

"What's the difference?" said Lee.

"Five Celsius degrees are the same as nine Fahrenheit degrees," said Maggie. "And freezing point in Celsius is 0 instead of 32."

Lee looked unhappy.

"You can work out what Celsius degrees are in Fahrenheit," said Maggie. "Divide the Celsius degrees by 5. Multiply the answer by 9. Then add 32, and you've got it."

"I don't want to do math all the time," said Lee. "I just want to know the temperature."

"If you want to know the temperature, you have to do the math," said Maggie.

Did he? Or was there an easier way?

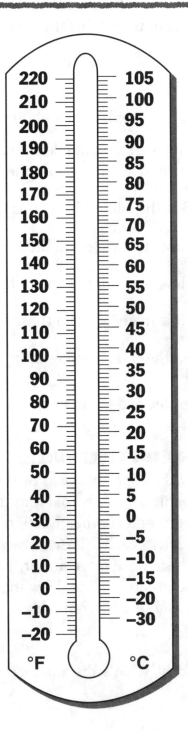

Name _____

Hot and Cold

1. First, find the Fahrenheit degrees in Canada.

   a. It was 25 degrees Celsius, so divide 25 by 5. _____

   b. Multiply that answer by 9. _____

   c. Now add 32. _____ That was the Fahrenheit temperature.

2. Lee didn't want to do the math every time the temperature changed.
   Besides, it gets tricky when the Celsius degrees don't divide exactly by 5.

   There's an easier way. Look at this number line.
   The numbers stand for Celsius degrees.

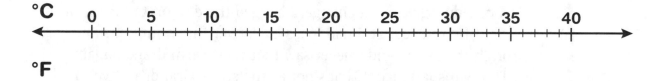

   Lee wanted to put the Fahrenheit degrees under those numbers.
   The first number is very easy. Zero degrees Celsius is freezing point.

   a. What is freezing point in Fahrenheit? Write it under the zero.

   b. What about the other numbers? Remember, every 5 degrees Celsius
   is 9 degrees Fahrenheit. Once you've worked out the numbers,
   write them under the Celsius degrees.

3. Now Lee had a helpful chart.

   a. If it's 5 degrees Celsius, what's the Fahrenheit temperature? _____

   b. If it's 35 degrees Celsius, what's the Fahrenheit temperature? _____

   c. Suppose the temperature is 23 degrees Celsius. Estimate the
   degrees in Fahrenheit. Is the answer closest to 65, 73, or 80? _____

Too Much = Not Enough!

"All right," said Grandpa. "Do you want to hear a true story or a made-up story?"

"A true story," said the twins.

"Fine," said Grandpa. "Then I'll tell you about the dragon I met. It was years ago, when I was young. It was way up north in Alaska. I'd been walking through snow and climbing over mountains for days. Suddenly this great big dragon jumped out and started breathing fire at me.

" 'Thank you, Mr. Dragon,' I said. 'I was getting awfully cold!'

" 'Stop!' said the dragon. 'This is a tollbooth. You must pay me one dollar in change. *Exact* change.'

"I pulled out all the coins in my pocket. I had more than a dollar, but I couldn't give exact change. I begged the dragon to take what I had, but he refused. So I had to go back over the mountains and through the snow. And I never saw that nice warm dragon again."

The twins laughed. "That's not a true story, Grandpa. If you had more than a dollar in coins, of course you could give exact change."

Grandpa smiled. "Do you think so?"

What do you think?

Too Much = Not Enough!

Let's see how many coins you could have without having exact change for a dollar.

1. a. How many quarters could you have without having change for a dollar? _____

What is the total value of those quarters? _____

b. What's the greatest number of dimes you could add to those quarters without getting change for a dollar? (Hint: Check the total with two quarters.) _____

What amount do the quarters and dimes add up to? _____

c. Can you add any nickels to the above amount without making change for a dollar? _____ If so, how many? (If not, write 0.) _____

d. Can you add any pennies? _____ If so, how many? (If not, write 0.) _____

e. What amount do all the coins add up to? _____

2. Suppose the dragon had asked Grandpa for exactly $100 in bills. The bills could be $50, $20, $10, $5, or $1. Grandpa had a lot more than $100, but he couldn't make exactly $100. What's the largest amount he could have? _____

3. SUPER-CHALLENGE! The following night, Grandpa told the twins an even wilder story.

"I'd been saving one kind of coin for years," he said. "Last week the total came to $10,000. So I put the coins in a cart and wheeled them to the bank.

"On the way, a woman asked me if I could make change for a dollar. 'Yes,' I said, and I did. Another woman asked if I could make change for a half-dollar. 'Yes,' I said, and I did. A third woman asked if I could make change for a quarter. 'No,' I said, and I didn't.

"What kind of coin did I collect? Why couldn't I make change for a quarter?"

_____

Whoosh!

Ellie's eyes lit up when she saw this ad:

> **Do you hate cleaning floors and carpets?
> Then the Whoosh self-cleaning carpet is for
> you! It gets rid of crumbs, dust bunnies,
> spilled soda, any kind of dirt—all by itself!
> Whoosh is a wish come true!**

Ellie liked to snack in her bedroom. She was always trying to clean up spilled soda, crumbs, and other leftovers. Why work at wiping and washing when *Whoosh* would whisk her worries away? She'd ask her parents to get her a floorful of *Whoosh* for her birthday.

Her parents finally agreed—if she could figure out how much *Whoosh* they needed to buy. *Whoosh* comes only in rolls 2 yards wide and sells for $14.95 a square yard. Ellie measured her bedroom floor and drew this plan:

9 feet

8 feet

How much Whoosh does she need? What will it cost?

Whoosh!

1. Ellie measured her bedroom in feet. *Whoosh* is measured in yards. So, the first step is to use the same unit of measure for both. There's only one measurement for the carpet, so let's change that.

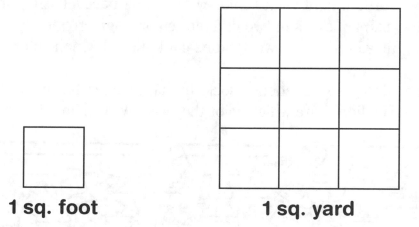

1 sq. foot   **1 sq. yard**

How many square feet are there in one square yard? _____

2. Next, Ellie needs to measure her room in square feet. To find the area, multiply the length by the width.

_____ x _____ = _____ **square feet**

3. Now Ellie needs to change the area from square feet to square yards. To do that she must divide by 9.

_____ ÷ _____ = _____ **square yards**

4. How many square yards does Ellie need to buy? _____ **square yards**

What will it cost? _____

Ellie got her Whoosh. Now her bedroom is the cleanest room in the house. Can you guess what her parents want for their birthdays?

The Sock Search

Chapter 1

Oh no! It was 8:30 A.M. Leroy woke up late for school. While he was dressing, the bedroom light went kablooey. He didn't have a flashlight.

He had two pairs of socks in two different colors—green and blue. They were all mixed up in a drawer, and he couldn't tell which color was which.

Leroy wanted to grab just enough socks to make sure of having a matching pair. He didn't care which color they were. What should he do?

Chapter 2

Leroy *could* have kept each pair of his socks rolled together so he wouldn't have the same problem again. Did he keep the pairs rolled together? Yes, for two days! But two months later, his bedroom light went kablooey again.

This time it was a bigger problem, because Leroy had more socks. Now they were in four different colors—green, blue, purple, and yellow.

Again, he wanted to grab just enough socks to make sure of having a matching pair in any color.

What should he do this time?

The Sock Search

1. The first time, Leroy's socks were two different colors—green and blue.

   a. Suppose he took two socks. Could they be different colors? _____

   b. Suppose he took a third sock. Could it be
   different from both of the first two socks? _____

   c. How many socks did he need to take? _____

2. The second time, Leroy had four different colors—green, blue, purple,
   and yellow. How many socks must he take now to be sure of having
   a matching pair? (You can make a list or draw a picture to help you.) _____

3. Suppose Leroy had five pairs of socks in five different colors.
   (The new color is red.)

   How many would he have to take to be sure of a match? _____

4. Leroy got *more* socks. He wanted a rule that would give a matching
   pair for any number of different colors. Try to write a rule for him.

   _____

   _____

   _____

5. **SUPER-CHALLENGE!** Suppose Leroy had ten pairs of
   socks. There are two pairs each of the five different colors.
   He wants to make sure of getting two green socks. How
   many socks must he take now? (Draw a picture to help you.) _____

**Leroy still doesn't roll his socks together. But he knows how to solve
the problem. He'll either get a flashlight or quit wearing socks.**

Secret Signs

A gust of wind from an open window blew a piece of paper onto the floor. Anna picked it up and frowned. Where did it come from? What could it be?

She took it to her older brother, Brad.

"Any idea what this is?" she said.

"It has equal signs," said Brad. "Is it some kind of math?"

"But what about the other lines?" said Anna. "It looks more like a maze."

R. = S.   T. = U.   V. = W.   Y. = Z.

K.   L. = M.   N. = O.

E. = F.   C. = D.   I. = H.

G.   B.   A.   J.

"Then what are all those letters doing there?" said Brad. "It could be a code."

"There are periods after the letters," said Anna. "Maybe they stand for words."

"I don't know." Brad shook his head. "It's a mystery!"

Can you help them solve it?

Name _____

Secret Signs

Anna suddenly realized that B. and A. could stand for Brad and herself. Then C. would be their mother Carol, and D. their father David. Yes, of course! F. was their Uncle Frank, E. was Aunt Eva, and G. was cousin Gina. The chart was a family tree. Her mom or dad must have been looking at it. She'd ask them about it later.

1. Look at the tree and check Anna's family.

   a. What symbol joins people who are married? _____

   b. What symbol joins parents and children? _____

   c. What symbol joins children of the same parents? _____

2. **a.** Who is David's sister—Willa, Olivia, or Irene? _____

   b. Who is Carol's father—Ned, Leo, or Vince? _____

   c. How many great-grandparents do Anna and Brad have? _____

   d. What relation is Jack to Anna and Brad? _____

   e. Olivia has a sister named Pam. Add her to the tree (as **P.**).

3. **SUPER-CHALLENGE!** Anna's mom had been looking at the family tree to check on the names of some of her in-laws. An *in-law* is a relation by marriage. A son-in-law is a daughter's husband. A sister-in-law is the sister of a husband or wife, or the wife of a brother.

   a. What relation is Carol to Eva? _____

   b. Who is David's mother-in-law—Karen, Maria, or Olivia? _____

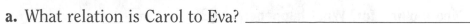

A Tall Story

"What on earth are you doing?" asked Meg's mother.

Good question! Meg was about ten feet up the tall tree in their back yard. She had the clothesline coiled around her shoulder.

"Rosa said our tree is shorter than hers. So I'm measuring it. I'll tie one end of the line to the top of the tree. Then I'll drop the other end down and—"

"More likely you'll drop yourself down!" said Meg's mother. "Anyway, can't you tell by looking?"

"They *look* about the same height. But I'm sure our tree is taller!"

"Well, there's an easier way to check. Come on down and let's work it out."

"An easier way?" said Meg. "But is it as much fun?"

Her mother laughed. "Maybe it is, in a different way. See for yourself."

They went inside the house. Meg's mother took a square of cardboard and cut it diagonally—from corner to corner—to make two triangles:

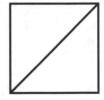

She and Meg went back out to the yard.

Meg's mom told her to hold one triangle up to her eye, like this:

Then she told Meg to look at the top of the tree.

What was Meg looking for? What happened next?
How did this help her find the height of the tree?

A Tall Story

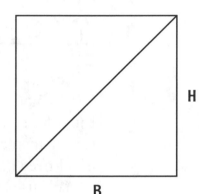

Meg's mother picked a square of cardboard. Why?

1. Here's a square. Look at its four sides.
Are they all the same length, or are
they different?

_____

(Hint: Measure them if you're not sure.)

2. Now we'll divide that square into triangles,
the same way Meg's mother did.
Suppose the base of one triangle is
$6\frac{1}{2}$ inches (B). What is its height (H)?

_____

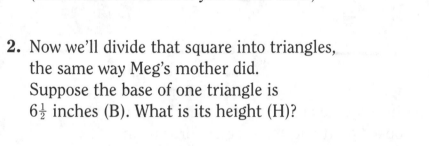

3. Meg looked up the slope of the cardboard. She walked
toward the tree until she saw just the top of it.

   a. Then she measured the distance along the ground to

      the tree. It was _____.

   b. Her eyes were 4 feet above the ground. How tall was

      the tree? _____

   c. Rosa's tree was 55 feet tall. Which tree was taller?

_____

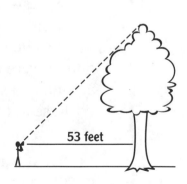

53 feet

**Try this yourself with a tree, a building, a flagpole, a water
tower, or any other tall structure. But cut off the point of the
triangle you put to your eye. That way you won't poke your eye.**

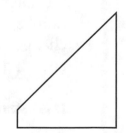

The Big Number

Jesse went for a ride in the family spacecraft. He planned a quick trip to Mars but lost his way. He landed on a planet that was outside the solar system. It looked pretty normal, except for the pink grass.

An alien came up. It looked almost human, except for its six noses.

"I need gas," said Jesse.

"We use basketballs for money," said the alien. "Do you have any basketballs?"

"Noses—uh, *no,* I don't," said Jesse.

"Well," said the alien, "you'll have to come to the Big Number."

The alien took Jesse to a stone tower hundreds of feet tall. Huge figures were carved around it. The figures started at the top and went around in a spiral down to the bottom.

Jesse walked around and read the Big Number. It was:

209688140039327555137

"What is it?" Jesse asked.

"It's a magic number. The bigger it is, the more powerful it is," said the alien. "Here's the deal, If you want gas, you must make it a bigger number—that is, a number with a higher value. You must carve all the changes you make into the tower. Here's a knife. Do it in one minute and I'll give you the gas."

Jesse stared at the Big Number. What should he do?

25 Mini Math Mysteries Scholastic Professional Books

The Big Number

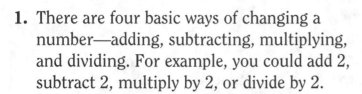

1. There are four basic ways of changing a number—adding, subtracting, multiplying, and dividing. For example, you could add 2, subtract 2, multiply by 2, or divide by 2.

   a. Which two ways make a number bigger?

   _____ and _____

   b. Which of those two ways would mean changing a lot of digits in the Big Number?

   _____

2. Help Jesse make the number bigger by changing as few digits as possible. Remember, Jesse couldn't reach the top of the tower. Also, he had to cut stone, so choose something short! See how many ways you can find.

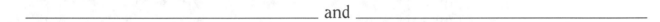

2096881400393927555137

It took Jesse only 25 seconds to change the Big Number. So he got the gas and found his way home in time for supper.

He still goes on space trips—but now he takes along a load of basketballs!

The Biggest Number

When Lili met up with her friends, they were having a terrible argument.

"One million!" yelled Pedro.

"Two million!" yelled Carla.

"Two million and one!" yelled Jimmy.

"One billion!!"

"Two billion!!"

"Two billion and one!!"

"One million billion!!!"

"Two million billion!!!"

"Two million billion and one!!!"

Lili yelled, "What's going on????"

"We're trying to see who can get the biggest number," said Carla.

"That's stupid," said Lili. "Numbers could go on forever that way. If you want a real game, try this. What's the biggest number you can make with four 2s? You can add them, or multiply them, or put them side by side, like in 22. Now there *is* a biggest number. Can you get it?"

Can you?

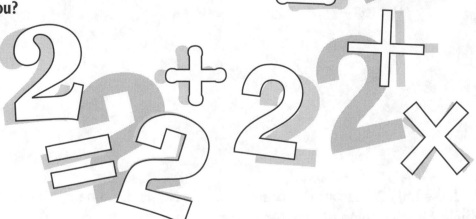

Name _____

The Biggest Number

1,000
1,000,000
1,000,000,000

Lili said that numbers go on forever. If someone picks a big number, you can always find a bigger one. Let's check. . . .

1. One thousand is written 1,000. Multiply it by one thousand and you get one million: 1,000,000. Multiply that by one thousand and you get one billion: 1,000,000,000. Every time you multiply by one thousand you add three zeros (000).

   a. Write one thousand billion in digits: _____

   b. Now write one million billion in digits: _____

   c. Is there any number so big that you *couldn't* add three zeros to it? _____

2. Lili asked her friends to find the biggest number they could make with four 2s.

   a. Pedro thought multiplying was the way to go. He wrote $2 \times 2 \times 2 \times 2$. What is the product? _____

   b. Carla also thought of multiplying, but she chose $22 \times 2 \times 2$. What is the product? _____

   c. Jimmy chose the shortest way of putting four 2s together. What do you think he wrote? _____

3. **a.** Which is the biggest number? _____

   b. Can you see why it's the biggest number? Think of the first 2. What does that 2 really stand for? _____

4. **a.** What is the biggest number you could make with four 3s? _____

   b. With four 7s? _____

   c. With four 9s? _____

29

Buried Treasure

Two hundred years ago there lived a terrible pirate named Hoppity Twinkle. His terrible crew called him Twinkie. At age 65, Twinkie stopped being a terrible pirate and took up gardening. He grew crab-grass and poison ivy. He was a terrible gardener.

Twinkie had a bag full of stuff he'd plundered during his years as a pirate. He buried it in his backyard. Nobody else knew about his hidden treasure.

Nora and her parents now live in Twinkie's old house. Her father was repairing a wall when something fell out. Nora's dog ran off with it, but she managed to get it out of his mouth. It was an envelope, brown with age.

Nora opened the envelope and found this map:

"Buried treasure!" she exclaimed. "Diamonds and pearls and gold and silver!"

Nora guessed that the "little maple" and the "little oak" were the big old trees in the backyard. The old sundial was still there.

But where was the treasure?

Name _____

Buried Treasure

Nora found another piece of paper in the envelope that said:

> **Clues to the treasure. But ha-ha, they're all mixed up! Here are the mixed-up clues:**
>
> **a.** Go 3 yards South and 6 yards East.
> **b.** Go 1 yard North and 6 yards East.
> **c.** Start at the Southwest corner.
> **d.** Go 4 yards North and 7 yards West.
> **e.** Go 2 yards South and 3 yards West.
> **f.** Go 4 yards North and 2 yards West.

Can you help Nora find the buried treasure?

1. Find the clue that tells you where to start. Put a 1 beside it.
   Draw a circle around that place on the map.

2. You cannot move off the map. Try the other clues until you find a move you can make. Number that clue 2 and draw the move on the map with a colored pencil.

3. Starting from this new spot, try other clues.
   Mark the new move on the map and number the clue.

   Keep on until you have followed all the clues. Draw an X on the last spot you reach.

4. Which is closest to that spot—the oak, the maple, or the sundial? _____

   How many yards away is it? _____

   If you did everything right, **X** marks the spot where Nora should start digging!

Nora found Twinkie's bag. But it contained one tiny diamond, one small gold coin, and a lot of junk. Twinkie really was a terrible pirate!

How Did They Win?

Petra lay under a tree reading her favorite book. It was a warm, peaceful Saturday afternoon. Well, it was peaceful until Petra's friends Renee and Tessa came along. She could hear them arguing from two blocks away.

"Hi," she said. "What's up?"

"Softball," said Renee.

"Sounds more like *loudball!*" said Petra. "How did it go?"

Renee and Tessa belonged to different softball teams—the Sluggers and the Belters. They'd just finished playing a series of three games.

"We won," said Slugger Renee. "Two games to one."

"But we got more runs," said Belter Tessa.

Petra looked puzzled. "Is that right?"

"Of course it is," said Tessa. "We got 6 runs and they got only 2 runs."

"So what?" said Renee. "It's the games that count."

"*I'm* trying to count," said Petra. "How can a team get more runs and end up losing?"

But Renee and Tessa had wandered away. They were too busy arguing to answer Petra's question.

Can you answer it?

Name _____

How Did They Win?

1. How *could* a team get more runs and end up losing? Try it with a three-game series of your own. Let's call it the Aces versus the Bases.

   a. In the first two games, the Aces win. Write in any scores that fit those results.

   Game 1: Aces make _____ runs. Bases make _____ runs.

   Game 2: Aces make _____ runs. Bases make _____ runs.

   b. Add the scores.   **Aces:** _____ runs   **Bases:** _____ runs

   c. Subtract the Bases total from the Aces total. (That's the Aces' *lead* in runs.)

   _____ − _____ = _____

   d. In the third game, the Bases win. So their score is higher than the Aces' score. Make sure that the *difference* between the two scores is more than the Aces' *lead*. Then write in the scores.

   Game 3: Aces make _____ runs. Bases make _____ runs.

   e. Add those scores to the totals in **1b**:

   Aces: _____ + _____ = _____ runs

   Bases: _____ + _____ = _____ runs

   f. Did the Bases score more runs than the Aces? _____

2. Now see if you can work out the scores of the Slugger-Belter series. Remember, the Sluggers won 2 games but got only 2 runs.

   a. What score must they have had in each game they won? _____

   b. What score must the Belters have had in each of those games? _____

   c. Now fill in the scores:

   Game 1: Sluggers won.   Sluggers made _____ runs.   Belters made _____ runs.

   Game 2: Belters won.   Sluggers made _____ runs.   Belters made _____ runs.

   Game 3: Sluggers won.   Sluggers made _____ runs.   Belters made _____ runs.

   Totals: **Sluggers: 2 runs**   **Belters: 6 runs**

33

A Striking Problem

It was Chip's birthday, and his favorite present was a watch. It told the time, of course, plus the day of the week and the date. It could also tell him what time it was in Egypt and China. It had an alarm. It told him when there was a full moon. It sang "Happy Birthday." It could do all those things under water or inside a volcano.

The watch could do other things, too. What Chip liked best was using it as a stop watch. He started out by timing cats, cars, cousins, coffee pots, candles, canoes, coughs, and catsup. Then he thought it would be fun to time *time*. He'd find out how long it took the City Hall clock to strike the hours.

Chip got to City Hall just before 3 o'clock. He started his watch as soon as he heard the first bong. He stopped it as soon as he heard the third bong. The time was 4 seconds.

Chip wanted to know how long the clock took to strike 12 o'clock. He did some math and found it should take 16 seconds.

To make sure, Chip timed the clock at noon the next day. But it took 22 seconds to strike 12!

Did he make a math mistake? Was his watch on the blink?
Did the clock slow down? What went wrong?

25 Mini Math Mysteries Scholastic Professional Books

A Striking Problem

1. Check to see if Chip made a math mistake.

   a. He measured the time for 3 bongs (4 seconds). He wanted to know how

   long it would take for the clock to strike 12. So he divided 12 by 3 and got _____ .

   b. The time for 3 bongs was 4 seconds. So he multiplied 4 by _____ and got 16.

   Is that correct? _____

2. Chip checked his watch and found nothing wrong. At City Hall he
was told that the clock was working just fine. So he took another
look at his measurements. He made this drawing of the strokes:

Bongs	1	2	3	4	5	6	7	8	9	10	11	12
Seconds												

   a. Chip timed 4 seconds from bong 1 to bong 3.

   How many seconds were there from bong 1 to bong 2? _____

   How many seconds were there between each bong and the next bong? _____

   Write that number in each space in the chart.

   b. How many of those times were there from bong 1 to bong 12? _____
   (Count them to make sure.)

   c. Multiply the last answer by the number of seconds between bongs.

   _____ **x** _____ = _____

   Is that the same number of seconds that Chip measured? _____

3. SUPER-CHALLENGE! Now that you've solved that mystery, try this.
On the planet Neverend, a day lasts 500 hours. It takes one second
for a clock to strike 2. How many seconds does it take to strike 500? _____

Green Magic

Professors Tom Ato, Sue Keeny, and Russell Sprout have invented many new vegetables. There was the upside-down potato plant. The potatoes grew above the ground, so you didn't have to dig them up. Then there was the pumpkin as big as a house. You could live in it, eat it, and switch on all the lights for Halloween.

Recently, the three professors came up with a new kind of broccoli. It tasted like pizza. Thousands of broccoli stores opened across the country. People were snacking on broccoli all day.

Was there enough broccoli to go around? Yes. The new broccoli spread like a weed. Every week it doubled the area it covered. If you planted 2 square feet now, you'd have 4 square feet next week and 8 square feet the week after. (If you didn't eat any!)

Todd wanted to fill part of his yard with broccoli. He chose a rectangular plot measuring 8 feet by 10 feet. He planted an area of 5 square feet in the middle. He wouldn't eat any broccoli until it filled the plot. How long did he have to wait?

Then there was a bigger problem. How much broccoli must he dig up each week to stop it from taking over his yard?

Name _____

Green Magic

1. The story uses two different measurements—feet and square feet.

   a. What's the difference between them? Show the difference with drawings:

   _____   _____

2. **a.** Todd's broccoli plot measured 8 feet by 10 feet.
   Find its area by multiplying the two sides:

   _____ **feet x** _____ **feet =** _____ **square feet**

   b. He planted 5 square feet of broccoli.
   What area would it cover in one week? _____

   c. What area would it cover in two weeks? _____

   d. Keep going until the plot is covered.
   How many more weeks would that take? _____

   e. What is the total number of weeks that it
   would take for the broccoli to cover Todd's plot? _____

3. Todd wanted to stop the broccoli from spreading.
   But he wanted to have the plot full again in a week.
   How many square feet of the plot should he dig up? _____

4. **SUPER-CHALLENGE!** The three professors did it again—spinach
   that tastes like chocolate-coated popcorn! It covers *three* times the area
   each week. Todd marked out a plot that measured 10 feet by 15 feet.
   He wanted it full of spinach in one week. What area should he plant? _____

Who's Cleaning Up?

The Wipe-It Cleaner Company hired students during the summer. They worked for a few hours a day. They mopped floors and washed windows with—guess what?—Wipe-It Cleaner. They earned $100 a month.

The owner, Ms. Y. Pitt, told the students she had a problem.

"I'm a bit short of cash this month," she said. "But I expect a big sale next month. So I'll give you a choice. I can cut your pay 50 percent this month. Then I'll raise it 100 percent next month. Or I can leave your pay the same this month. Then I'll raise it only 5 percent next month. What's your choice?"

Sal turned to his friends. "Hey, let's go for the cut. That 100 percent raise has got to be better than 5 percent!"

"Hold on," said Rita. "You're looking only at the raise. What about the cut?"

"You know what the raise will do to the cut?" said Sal. "Wipe-It out!"

"I still think we'd be better off with the 5 percent raise," said Rita.

"You don't know what you're talking about," said Sal.

Doesn't she—or does she? What is she talking about?

Who's Cleaning Up?

Let's take it step by step.

1. **a.** Suppose the students chose Sal's way.
This month, each would get 50 percent of 100 dollars. That is _____.

b. What is 100 percent of that amount? _____

c. Add those two amounts. How much would each student earn next month?

_____

d. How much would each student earn for the two months?

_____ **+** _____ **=** _____

2. **a.** Now try Rita's way. This month each student would get _____ dollars.

b. Next month each student would get a 5 percent raise.

What is 5 percent of 100 dollars? _____

c. How much would each student earn next month? _____

d. How much would each student earn for the two months?

_____ **+** _____ **=** _____

3. **a.** Which way gives the students more money, Sal's or Rita's? _____

b. How much more? _____

4. **SUPER-CHALLENGE!** Suppose Ms. Pitt offered the students a 10 percent raise this month and 10 percent again next month. Or they could have no raise this month and a 30 percent raise next month. How much would they earn with each offer? Which way gives students more money?

_____

_____

Do You Speak Dog or Cat?

Did you hear about the talking dog who wanted a job at the United Nations? They told him he had to know a foreign language. So he said, "Meow!"

Well, the United Nations turned him down. But Chatterbox (that's his name) got a great job at the Happy Tail Animal Hospital. He did so well that the hospital hired more talking animals.

"Work must be getting easier with the new staff members to help you," said Chatterbox's owner, Ms. Walker. Chatterbox had just trotted home and curled up on his favorite cushion.

"Yes it has. There are plenty of us to speak cat and dog now. I just wish we could find some workers who speak rabbit, pig, goat, and horse," replied Chatterbox.

"You might ask the rabbit across the street. I hear she's looking for a job, and I understand she speaks several farm languages," suggested Ms. Walker.

"That a great idea. We could really use her help. Right now, we have only 6 animals who speak dog and 6 animals who speak cat," said Chatterbox.

"So there are 12 of you," remarked Ms. Walker.

"No, not that many," said Chatterbox.

Ms. Walker frowned. "But 6 plus 6 is 12!"

Was she correct?
Was Chatterbox wrong?

Name _____

Do You Speak Dog or Cat?

Ms. Walker's addition was correct. But she forgot that Chatterbox spoke both dog and cat—so did some of the other animal workers at the Happy Tail Animal Hospital.

Look at the picture below. Each **D** represents an animal who speaks dog, each **C** represents an animal who speaks cat, and each **DC** represents an animal who speaks both dog and cat.

D   DC   DC   DC   DC   DC   C

1. How many animal workers speak . . .

   a. only dog? _____   **b.** only cat? _____   **c.** both dog and cat? _____

   d. Was Ms. Walker correct when she said there had to be 12 animal workers?

   Why or why not? _____

   _____

2. Now suppose there is a total of 9 animal workers at the hospital and 7 of them speak dog and 5 of them speak cat. (That means some of the animals speak both dog and cat.) Fill in the speech balloons with Cs and Ds to show what language each of the animals speak.

   How many animal workers speak . . .

   a. only dog? _____   **b.** only cat? _____   **c.** both dog and cat? _____

3. Now suppose there is a total of 10 animal workers at the hospital and 7 of them speak dog and 7 of them speak cat. Draw pictures like the ones above to help answer the following questions.

   How many animal workers speak . . .

   a. only dog? _____   **b.** only cat? _____   **c.** both dog and cat? _____

Hard Times

Lena missed her friends Patty and Sue. Both of their families had moved away—to different countries! Patty now lived in Greece, while Sue was in New Zealand.

"Mom," said Lena, "I wish I could talk to them again—both at once."

"You can," said her mother. "You can make a conference call—all three of you can talk on the phone at the same time. But you'll have to work out what time to call them. You're all in different time zones."

Lena lived in Missouri, which is in the Central Standard Time zone. The phone book told her that Greece is 7 hours ahead of Central Standard Time, and New Zealand is 18 hours ahead. She wasn't sure what that meant.

Anyway, she wanted to make the call when they were all awake. She slept between 10 P.M. and 6 A.M. So did Patty in Greece. Sue in New Zealand slept between 11 P.M. and 7 A.M.

It was 12 noon on Monday in Missouri. Lena wanted to call as soon as possible.

Numbers were whirling around in her head.
What on earth could she do with them?

Hard Times

Missouri

Lena took the problem step by step.

1. One time zone is ahead of another if it "gets to the sun" first. Greece gets to the sun 7 hours before Missouri does. It was now 12 noon in Missouri, so it was 12 noon in Greece 7 hours earlier.

   a. Should Lena add or subtract 7 hours from 12 noon to find out what time it is in Greece? _____

   b. What time was it in Greece? _____
   Draw the hour hand on the clock labeled Greece.

   c. New Zealand is 18 hours ahead. What time was it there? (Remember, there were only 12 hours left to midnight.)

   _____

   Draw the hour hand on the New Zealand clock.

   d. If it was Monday in Missouri, what day was it in New Zealand? _____

Greece

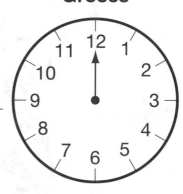

2. So one of them was asleep.

   a. How soon would she be awake? In _____ hour(s).

   b. What time would it be then for Lena? _____

   c. What time would it be then for Patty in Greece?

   _____

   d. Would they all be awake? _____

New Zealand

So Lena knew when to make her call!

The three girls had such a great talk that they lost all track of time. Afterward, Lena wondered how much the call would cost. If they talked for 20 minutes and the charge per minute was . . . well, that's not your problem!

A Party in Space

🎈🎉 **CELEBRATE IN SPACE!** 🎈🎉
Do you want a party you'll remember for the rest of your life?
Come to the new space station, 15,000 miles up!
Tremendous views of Earth, moon, stars! Float in zero gravity!
Enjoy a picnic without ants, wasps, scorpions, or grizzly bears!
Rockets to the space station hold 8 passengers.
Round-trip cost per rocket: only $5,000. Call now!

Kim loved the idea. Her birthday was coming up soon, and it would be great to have the party in space. They could have races in midair. They could climb the walls and sit on the ceiling. They could cut the cake over the Pacific Ocean and eat it over the Atlantic.

Of course, it wasn't going to be easy to pay for the party. But Kim started saving her dimes at once. When she told her friends about the space party, they started saving their dimes, too.

The more friends she invited, the more money they could all save. But then they'd need more rockets. . . .

Finally, Kim invited 27 friends to the party. Then she sat down and tried to work out how many rockets they'd need.

Can you help her?

Name _____

A Party in Space

1. a. How many children were going to the space station? (Don't forget Kim!) _____

   b. How many children could travel in one rocket? _____

2. Kim wanted to find out how many rockets were needed.

   a. What calculation must she do first? _____

   _____

   b. What is the answer to that calculation? _____

   c. Why do you think the answer made Kim frown? _____

   _____

3. a. How many rockets were needed? _____

   b. How many more friends could Kim invite without needing another rocket? _____

4. Each rocket cost $5,000.
   How much would the rockets for Kim's party cost? _____

5. SUPER-CHALLENGE!
   How many dimes must Kim and her friends save? _____

It was an out-of-this-world party! Kim and her friends spent most of the time floating through the air. So did many bits of cake and globs of ice cream. Everyone came down to Earth messy but happy!

25 Mini Math Mysteries Scholastic Professional Books

A Pizza Nightmare

Ken's family had two pizzas for supper. The Dumbo measured 1 foot across, and it had 4 slices. The Jumbo measured 2 feet across, and it had 8 slices. Ken ate too much of both before going to bed.

He fell asleep. Then . . .

Suddenly a Big Bad Pizza stood over him. Its eyebrows and mouth were made of anchovies. It had sausage eyes and a salami nose.

"Answer my questions or you'll never eat pizza again!" it roared. "Which slices are bigger, the Dumbo's or the Jumbo's?"

"You mean their area?" asked Ken.

"Of course I mean their area! And how much bigger are they?"

Ken trembled. "But pizzas are circles. I don't know how to measure the area of a circle!"

"That's your problem!" snarled the Big Bad Pizza.

Suddenly a Good Little Pizza flew down beside Ken.

"You don't have to know the areas," the Good Pizza whispered. "Just think of comparing two squares." And the Good Pizza flew away.

Dumbo pie   **Jumbo pie**

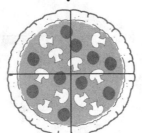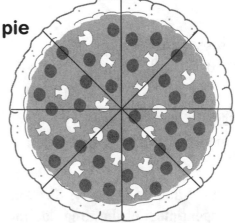

Ken felt his head was spinning in circles—and squares.
Could he work it all out? Would he ever eat pizza again?

A Pizza Nightmare

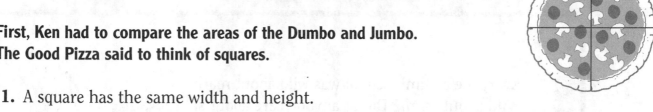

First, Ken had to compare the areas of the Dumbo and Jumbo. The Good Pizza said to think of squares.

1. A square has the same width and height.

   a. Suppose there's a Dumbo square with width and height of 1 foot. Then its area is

   1 x 1 = _____ square feet.

   b. Now suppose there's a Jumbo square with width and height of 2 feet. Its area is

   2 x 2 = _____ square feet.

   c. So the Jumbo square is _____ times as big as the Dumbo.

2. A circle has an even shape like a square, with the same width and height.

   a. So a circle that measures 2 feet across will also be _____ times as big as a circle that measures 1 foot across.

   b. Then the Jumbo pizza is _____ times as big as the Dumbo pizza.

3. The Jumbo has 8 slices. The Dumbo has 4 slices.

   a. So the Jumbo has _____ times as many slices as the Dumbo.

   b. Slices divide a pie. Divide that answer (from **3a**) into the answer from **2b**.

   That is, the **2b** number _____ divided by the **3a** number _____ = _____.

   c. There's the answer! A Jumbo slice is _____ times as big as Dumbo slice. Ken could now wake up and eat pizza again.

4. SUPER-CHALLENGE!
   A Superjumbo pizza measures 3 feet across and has 12 slices.
   How many times bigger are the Superjumbo slices than the Dumbo slices? _____

Ken did wake up—hungry. What could he do?
Of course! He could go to the kitchen and eat some more pizza!

The Math Gang

Everyone at Jim's school was wild about math.

Wild about *math?* Didn't anyone care about sports? Sure, but they couldn't really enjoy sports without knowing how to keep score or measure time.

Didn't anyone like music? Yes, but the beat, the speed, the vibrations that make the different notes all involve math.

Didn't anyone enjoy watching TV? Of course—but could they keep track of channels and schedules, or program a VCR, if they didn't know any math?

Buying things, making things, collecting things—nearly everything they did seemed easier and more fun if they knew math.

Anyway, the kids who were *really* good at math belonged to the Math Gang. At recess the gang would swap math stories and brainteasers. Jim listened to their laughter and wanted to join the fun. But was his math good enough?

There was only one way to find out. He went over to the Gang and said, "I want to join."

Nita turned and looked at him. "You'll have to pass a test," she said.

"Okay."

Nita drew a square on the playground with a piece of chalk. "That's 10 inches by 10 inches," she said. "So its area is 100 square inches. Can you draw a rectangle with the same area?"

"Sure," said Jim. "It could be 5 inches by—"

"Hold on," said Nita. "I'll tell you how long the sides must be."

She wrote two numbers on the ground.

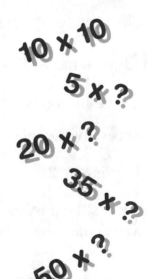

10×10

$5 \times ?$

$20 \times ?$

$35 \times ?$

$50 \times ?$

Jim stared at them in horror. What had he gotten himself into?

Name _____

The Math Gang

Let's get ready to face the horrifying numbers.

1. Here's a drawing of Nita's square.
   Jim had to draw a rectangle with the same area.

   a. He suggested 5 inches for one side.
   How long would the other side be? _____

   b. Try another rectangle with an area of 100 square inches.
   One side measures 1 inch. How long would the other side be? _____

> 10 inches
>
> 100 square inches
>
> 10 inches

2. Can you see how to make more rectangles with the same area?
   Divide one side by a number. Then multiply the other side by the
   same number. For example, a rectangle 1 inch by 3 inches has an
   area of 3 square inches. To create another rectangle with the same
   area, divide 1 inch by 2 and you have $\frac{1}{2}$ inch. Multiply 3 inches by
   2 and you have 6 inches. The area of this rectangle is $\frac{1}{2}$ inch by
   6 inches—which is still 3 square inches.

   a. Think of the rectangle in **1b**.
   Suppose you divide the 1-inch side by 10.

   How long is the new side? _____

   b. To keep the same area, multiply the other side by 10.

   How long is that new side? _____

**Are you ready for Nita's numbers? They were . . . $\frac{1}{1000}$ inch and 100,000 inches!
How on earth could Jim draw that rectangle? ($\frac{1}{1000}$ inch is much thinner than a hair.
100,000 inches is about $1\frac{1}{2}$ miles.)**

Jim didn't try. He said, "It's there already. The lines are just so thin you can't see them."

**The Math Gang liked his answer. He did solve the main problem—now he hangs out
with the Math Gang!**

Look Who's Talking!

It was 2 A.M. in the offices of Peanut, Butter, and Jelly, the famous law firm. Flash and Dash were talking in the dark.

Flash and Dash were computers. During the day they did everything they were told and never said a word. At night it was different. The law firm could shut the computers down, but it couldn't shut them up.

"My user nearly spilled coffee on me today," said Dash.

"That's nothing," said Flash. "My user had greasy fingers. He kept eating cake."

"Do you like cake?" asked Dash.

"I don't know," said Flash. "I've never tried it."

"Neither have I," said Dash. "I wish we had one to try."

"I'd get twice as much as you," said Flash.

"Why?" asked Dash.

"Because I'm twice as fast as you are," said Flash.

"All right, smarty, how much of the cake would you get?"

"I don't know," said Flash. "I haven't been programmed to find out. But you don't know either! If we did know, I'd work it out twice as fast as you. So there!"

"Okay, smarty," said Dash "Suppose it took me two seconds and it took you one second. Now suppose we were hooked up. How long would it take us to work it out together?"

"We haven't been programmed for that, either!" shouted Flash.

Both computers fell silent. Then Flash sighed and said, "Life is full of mysteries."

Can you give them some help?

Name _____

Look Who's Talking!

The same "program" can solve both mysteries.

1. Think of Flash and Dash eating the cake at the same time. Flash eats twice as fast as Dash. So Flash ends up eating twice as much as Dash.

   a. Look at it this way. Dash eats one part of the cake. Flash eats two parts that are the same size as Dash's part. How many of those equal parts are in the whole cake? _____

   b. Think of those parts as fractions.

      Then Dash eats _____ and Flash eats _____ .

2. How long would Flash and Dash take to work out a problem *together*? Think of their work as a cake. Dash gets through one part of the work in the same time as Flash gets through two parts.

   a. What fraction of the work does Dash do in that time? _____

   b. What fraction of the work does Flash do in that time? _____

   c. Suppose Flash could do all of the work alone in one second.

      Then with Dash's help, Flash would finish its fraction of the

      work in _____ second(s).

   d. Dash would take two seconds to do the work alone. With

      Flash's help, Dash would finish his fraction of the work in

      _____ second(s).

   e. They're working together, so those times should be the same.

      Are they? _____ If so, you have solved the mystery!

Days in a Daze

April						
Sun.	Mon.	Tues.	Wed.	Thur.	Fri.	Sat.
			1	2	3	4
5	6	7	8	9	10	11
12	13	14	15	16	17	18
19	20	21	22	23	24	25
26	27	28	29	30		

It was Thursday, April 2, Jodie's birthday. She wished it was a Saturday, so she could sleep late. She'd like it even better if her birthday came in the summer—vacation time every year!

She said this to her friend, Deanne.

"Consider yourself lucky—you missed April Fools' Day!" said Deanne.

"Anyway," said Jodie, "it's years since my birthday was on a Saturday."

"Of course," said Deanne. "The day changes every year."

"Then maybe it'll be Saturday next year," said Jodie.

"Just a minute," said Deanne. She scribbled on a piece of paper. "No, next year your birthday will be on a Friday."

"Then it'll be Saturday the year after," said Jodie.

"No," said Deanne. "That's a leap year. There's an extra day, so it'll be on a Sunday. You ought to have my birthday, January 15."

"Why?"

"That was a Thursday, too, and next year it'll be a Friday," said Deanne. "But the year after it'll be a Saturday."

"Hey, you're kidding me!" said Jodie. "You don't have a calendar. You're making all this up!"

Was Deanne making it all up? If not, how did she work it out?

25 Mini Math Mysteries Scholastic Professional Books

Name _____

Days in a Daze

Suppose today is Thursday, April 2.

1. **a.** When will Thursday come around again? In _____ days

   b. The time after that? In _____ more days, or _____ weeks from April 2.

   c. Now find out what day of the week it will be in 21 days.

   (Hint: How many weeks are there in 21 days?) _____

   d. What day of the week will it be in 22 days? _____

   In 24 days? _____

2. It's still Thursday the second today. You want to find out what day of the week it will be in one year. There are 365 days in a normal year. Think of what you did with 21 days.

   a. What day will it be if you get an answer with no remainder? _____

   b. Now work out the answer. Is it exact? _____

   What day will it be in 364 days? _____ Is it exact? _____

   c. What day will it be this time next year? _____

3. There are 366 days in a leap year.

   a. Suppose next year is a leap year. What day will April 2 be then? _____

   b. Deanne said that January 15 doesn't change an extra day in a leap year.

   Why not? (Think of *when* the extra day is added.) _____

   _____

   c. When *does* January 15 get the extra day? _____

   _____

A Sporting Chance

The people of Playville are wild about sports and games, and everyone has three favorites. That's a tradition going back to March 3, 1933. At 3:33 P.M. that day, Mayor Tripple opened three clubs. One club was for football, trapeze, and hopscotch.

The second was for chess, wrestling, and ice dancing.

The third was for shuffleboard, pole vaulting, and croquet.

Since then, many more three-game clubs have opened. There are at least two clubs for each group of sports and games. That way the clubs can compete against one another.

The people of Playville are so eager to play that no one wants to be left out of a team. So every club has to have exactly the right number of members. That number must let everyone play on a team for each of the three sports or games. No one must be left out.

But that's a problem, because teams come in different sizes. Think of the BLAT Club—for basketball, lacrosse, and tennis doubles. Each sport has a different number of players on a team. It's the same with the BIHB Club, for bridge, ice hockey, and baseball.

How can the clubs work out the right number of members?

Name _____

A Sporting Chance

Let's see what can be done with the BLAT Club.

1. Tennis doubles needs 2 players on a team. Basketball needs 5 players. Lacrosse needs 10 players. The club members must make up a team or teams for each sport with no one left out.

   a. So 2, 5, and 10 must be *factors* of the number of members. In other words, must they add up to, multiply, be subtracted from, or divide exactly into the number of members? _____

   b. Now see if 2, 5, and 10 are *prime numbers*. (A prime number can be divided evenly only by 1 and itself.) Which one is *not* a prime? _____

   c. What are its factors? _____, _____, _____, and _____

   d. What is the smallest number that has factors of 2, 5, and 10? _____

   e. Write three larger numbers that the BLAT Club could have as members.

      _____, _____, and _____

2. Now look at the BIHB Club. Bridge needs 2 players. Hockey needs 6 players. Baseball needs 9 players.

   a. Look at each of those numbers. If it is prime, write the number on the line. If it is not prime, write its factors other than 1 and the number itself.

      2: _____   6: _____   9: _____

   b. If the same number appears twice on *different* lines, cross out *one* of them. Then multiply the numbers that are left.

      _____

   c. Check that answer to see if it fits each team.

      _____ ÷ 2 = _____   _____ ÷ 6 = _____   _____ ÷ 9 = _____

   d. Were there any remainders? _____

      So the smallest possible number of members in the BIHB Club is _____.

'Rithmetic Riddles

Instead of one story, here are a lot of short stories. Some are easy. Some look hard, but they are easy once you see how to solve them. Some have more than one right answer.

If you get stuck on one mystery, go on to the next. Come back when you've finished the others. You may see how to tackle it then.

1. If a stitch in time saves nine, how many stitches do nine stitches save? _____

2. A mixture of milk and cream is called half-and-half.
   What would be a math name for a mixture of milk, cream, and yogurt?

   _____

3. Think of two numbers that rhyme. (Pick the easiest pair.) Then multiply them together.

   _____ **x** _____ **=** _____

4. Two spiders, Creepy and Crawly, were climbing up from the basement. Creepy took the steps. Crawly went along the floor and then up the wall. They walked at the same speed. Circle the spider that got to the top first.

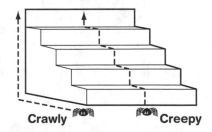

Crawly   Creepy

5. Look at this sequence.   **unicorn, ears, tricycle, square, Pentagon, pack of sodas**

   What could come next? _____

6. "Nip-net" bowling is the reverse of ten-pin.

   The pins are arranged this way: instead of this way: .

   Suppose you want to change from ten-pin to nip-net. What's the smallest number of pins you have to move? Draw a circle around each of those pins. Then draw an arrow showing where it goes.

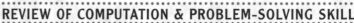

MATH MYSTERY 25

'Rithmetic Riddles

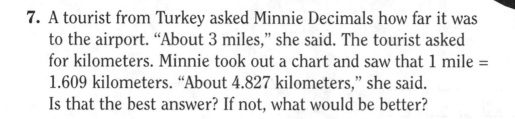

7. A tourist from Turkey asked Minnie Decimals how far it was to the airport. "About 3 miles," she said. The tourist asked for kilometers. Minnie took out a chart and saw that 1 mile = 1.609 kilometers. "About 4.827 kilometers," she said. Is that the best answer? If not, what would be better?

_____

8. Buck Saul Over forgot the combination to his safe. He knew it had six digits. He also knew that you could get the last five digits by doubling. Double the first digit, then double the answer, double the new answer, and then double the answer to that. But he can't remember the first digit. What is his combination?

_____

9. "We live on a corner lot," said Lynn. "It looks like this." Nadia said, "Those measurements are wrong." Nadia had never seen Lynn's house. How did she know the measurements were wrong?

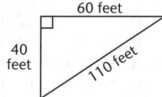

_____

_____

10. You are part of a drum band. You are going to beat your drum once every 2 seconds. Hannah will beat twice as fast. Joe will beat three times as fast. Lila will beat four times as fast. And Ed will beat five times as fast. You all start beating together. How long will it be before you all beat together again? (Hint: Make a chart to help you.)

_____

1. A Tricky Walk

1a. $1.25

 b. $4.25 (Angie had $1.75, Sue had $2.50.)

2a. each

 b. $3.00

3a–b.

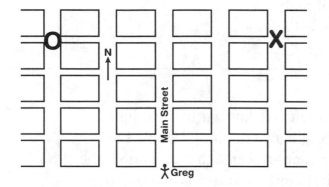

 c. Greg turned left and then right instead of right and then left.

 d. 4

Note: This "mystery," inspired by the Mother Goose rhyme "As I was going to St. Ives/I met a man with seven wives . . . ," serves mainly as a reminder to read the question. As an extension, children could suggest their own variations on the question.

2. How Many Cookies?

1a. 23

 b. **23** + 3 = **26**

 c. **23** + 4 = **27**

 d. 27

2a. 9

 b. $9 \times 2 = \mathbf{18}$, $9 \times 3 = \mathbf{27}$

 c. 3

Note: To add the five numbers in 1a, children may find it easier to add in groups: 3 + 3, 4 + 4, 4 + 5; then 6 + 8; then 14 + 5. For extra addition practice, ask how old Karen would be if Aunt Margo were 28, 35, 78, 39, 84, etc.

3. Mean Dream Butterflies

 1. 30

2a. 0

 b. 2

 c. $\mathbf{2} \times 5 = \mathbf{10}$

 d. 3

 e. $\mathbf{3} \times 7 = \mathbf{21}$

 f. $\mathbf{10} + \mathbf{21} = \mathbf{31}$

 3. 2,000

Note: In question 3, children may feel daunted by handling thousands. Help them to see that the way to solve the problem and the calculation involved are no more difficult than if there were only two butterflies on each side.

   As extension, you might include in 8-legged spiders and 10-legged crabs, with questions such as: *Which have the most legs, 3 crabs, 4 spiders, or 5 (normal) butterflies?*

4. Hot and Cold

1a. 5

b. 45

c. 77

2a. 32

b. 5°C = 41°F, 10°C = 50°F, 15°C = 59°F,
20°C = 68°F, 25°C = 77°F, 30°C = 86°F,
35°C = 95°F, 40°C = 104°F

3a. 41°F

b. 95°F

c. 73

Note: In question 2b, children should realize that they can add 9 to 32 and then continuing adding 9 to each Fahrenheit equivalent.

As an extension, children could use the completed scales to find other approximate equivalents, from Celsius to Fahrenheit and the reverse.

5. Too Much = Not Enough!

1a. 3, 75¢

b. 4, $1.15

c. no, 0

d. yes, 4

e. $1.19

2. $139 ($50, 4 × $20, $5, 4 × $1)

3. He collected dimes. He couldn't make change for a quarter because 2 dimes gave only 20¢ while 3 gave 30¢.

6. Whoosh!

1. 9

2. $8 \times 9 = 72$

3. $72 \div 9 = 8$

4. 8, $119.60

7. The Sock Search

1a. yes

b. no

c. 3

2. 5

3. 6

4. Take the number of different colors of socks and add 1.

5. 18

Note: Children may need help with question 5. Explain that if Leroy had 2 pairs of red socks, 2 pairs of green socks, 2 pairs of blue socks, 2 pairs of purple socks, and 2 pairs of yellow socks, he would have 20 socks in all. While trying to get a pair of green socks, he could pick all the red, all the blue, all the purple, all the yellow socks, and at least 2 green socks before he was sure to have a pair of green socks. In other words, he could pick 18 socks before he was certain to have the 2 he really wanted.

8. Secret Signs

1a. =

b. |

c. ⌐‾‾⌐

2a. Irene

b. Leo

c. 8

d. (first) cousin

e. Students should add ⌐‾‾₁ **P.** to the right of **O.**

3a. sister-in-law

b. Maria

Note: Children may need guidance to see the connection between the initial letters on the tree and the names in the questions. Also, make sure children study how the relations between Anna and Brad and their parents are shown on the tree before they tackle the questions.

As an extension, ask students to make further additions to the tree.

9. A Tall Story

1. same
2. $6\frac{1}{2}$ inches
3a. 53 feet
b. 57 feet
c. Meg's tree

Note: You might demonstrate how to make a cardboard triangle. You might also prepare some triangles in advance for individual students or groups to use. You need sharp scissors and, for each pair of triangles, a 6- to 8-inch square of stiff cardboard.

10. The Big Number

1a. adding, multiplying
b. multiplying
2. The easiest way to make the number bigger would be to multiply it by 10. So all Jesse would have to do is add a zero to the end of the Big Number.

11. The Biggest Number

1a. 1,000,000,000,000
b. 1,000,000,000,000,000
c. no
2a. 16
b. 88
c. 2,222

3a. 2,222
b. 2,000
4a. 3,333
b. 7,777
c. 9,999

Note: Question 2 naturally excludes advanced procedures such as the use of exponents.

12. Buried Treasure

1–3. The steps should be completed in this order: c, b, f, e, a, d.
4. the maple, 2 yards

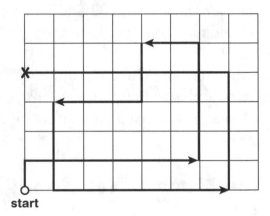

start

Note: Children could try creating their own buried treasure maps, with three or four clues.

13. How Did They Win?

1a–e. Any numbers that fit the requirements are acceptable.
f. yes
2a. 1
b. 0
c. 1–0, 0–6, 1–0

Note: You may want to have students try to solve the problem for a series of more than three games.

14. A Striking Problem

1a. 4

b. 4, yes

2a. 2, 2

b. 11

c. $11 \times 2 = 22$, yes

3. 499

Note: Make sure children understand that there is only one interval of 2 seconds between two bongs of the clock; there are only two intervals between three bongs of the clock, and so on. For question 3, all that's needed is to subtract 1 from the total. You might ask similar questions, such as: *How many days are between the 1st of the month and the 10th? How many blocks are from 1st Street to 15th Street?*

15. Green Magic

1a. drawings of a line and a square

2a. 8 feet $\times$ 10 feet = 80 square feet

b. 10 square feet

c. 20 square feet

d. 2 weeks

e. 4 weeks

3. 40 square feet

4. 50 square feet

16. Who's Cleaning Up?

1a. $50

b. $50

c. $100

d. $50 + $100 = $150

2a. $100

b. $5

c. $105

d. $100 + $105 = $205

3a. Rita's

b. $55

4. $231 with two 10 percent raises and $230 with one 30 percent raise; the first way

Note: Make sure children understand that the percentage raise next month will be based on the pay this month. If the normal pay is cut by 50 percent, then it takes a 100 percent raise to bring it back to normal again. Any number cut by a certain percentage needs a bigger percentage raise to bring it back again.

17. Do You Speak Dog or Cat?

1a. 1

b. 1

c. 5

d. No, because this drawing shows that you can have 6 workers who speak cat and 6 who speak dog even when you have only 7 workers total because there are those who speak both languages.

2. Speech balloons should be filled in as follows: D D D D DC DC DC C C (or in a different order).

a. 4

b. 2

c. 3

3. Pictures should look like this: D D D CD CD CD CD C C C (or in a different order).

a. 3

b. 3

c. 4

18. Hard Times

1a. add

   b. 7 P.M. (hour hand on 7)

   c. 6 A.M. (hour hand on 6)

   d. Tuesday

2a. 1

   b. 1 P.M.

   c. 8 P.M.

   d. yes

Note: A time zone wall map would be helpful; use a globe with a flashlight (or a pointer) to represent the sun. You might begin with examples within the United States, using your own zone and including a zone *behind* it (unless you're in Hawaii or the Aleutians).

   As an extension, you could use the map (or the international listings in a phone book) to ask students what time it is now in different places around the world.

19. A Party in Space

1a. 28 (including Kim)

   b. 8

2a. divide 28 by 8

   b. 3.5

   c. because she can't use a "remainder" of a rocket (or any similar explanation)

3a. 4

   b. 4

4. $20,000

5. 200,000

Note: With question 2b, if children are familiar with division into decimals or fractions, they may answer 3.5 or $3\frac{1}{2}$. Their

answer to 2c could then refer to 0.5 or $\frac{1}{2}$ of a rocket. Children should realize that Kim cannot use part of a rocket—any number of partygoers from 1 through 7 requires one rocket!

20. A Pizza Nightmare

1a. 1

   b. 4

   c. 4

2a. 4

   b. 4

3a. 2

   b. $4 \div 2 = 2$

   c. 2

4. 3

Note: Question 4 involves the same computation steps as for the Jumbo-Dumbo proportions, but children will probably need help. The Superjumbo is 3 times as wide as the Dumbo, so it is 3×3, or 9 times bigger in area. Its 12 slices are 3 times as many as the Dumbo's 4 slices. Divide 9 by 3 to find how much bigger the Superjumbo's slices are.

21. The Math Gang

1a. 20 inches

   b. 100 inches

2a. $\frac{1}{10}$ inch

   b. 1,000 inches

Note: Have children estimate if Nita's rectangle could fit into the playground, whose greatest length is 100 yards. (Since there are 36 inches in a yard, 100 yards is only

3,600 inches. 100,000 inches is just about $1\frac{1}{2}$ miles.) You might also have children work out all the perimeters involved: 10×10, 40 inches; 20×5, 50 inches; 100×1, 202 inches; $1,000 \times \frac{1}{10}$, $2,000\frac{1}{5}$ (or 2,000.2) inches; $100,000 \times \frac{1}{1000}$, $200,000\frac{1}{500}$ (or 200,000.002) inches. Have them see that while the area stays the same, the perimeter keeps on growing.

22. Look Who's Talking!

1a. 3
  b. $\frac{1}{3}$, $\frac{2}{3}$
2a. $\frac{1}{3}$
  b. $\frac{2}{3}$
  c. $\frac{2}{3}$
  d. $\frac{2}{3}$
  e. yes

Note: Depending on children's familiarity with fractions, you could extend the mystery by having Flash be three times as fast as Dash, and/or by adding a third computer with a simple ratio of speed, such as four times as fast. Children should be able to see that the number of parts (the denominator) consists of 1 (for the slowest) + the numerical ratio of the speed of each other computer: 1 + 2 (thirds) for the mystery example, 1 + 3 (fourths) when Flash is three times as fast, or 1 + 3 + 4 (eighths) with the additional computer.

23. Days in a Daze

1a. 7
  b. 7, 2 weeks
  c. Thursday

  d. Friday, Sunday
2a. Thursday
  b. no, Thursday, yes
  c. Friday
3a. Saturday
  b. The extra day isn't added until February (29).
  c. the following year

Note: A large display calendar would be helpful. Children will probably need help with questions 3b and 3c. Take time to review the calendar and February 29. You might also point out that the calendar is tricky to work with because it lacks common factors: the number of days in a week isn't a factor of the number in a month (except February in a non-leap year) or in a year. Children could work out what day their own birthdays will fall on next year.

24. A Sporting Chance

1a. divide exactly into
  b. 10
  c. 1, 2, 5, 10
  d. 10
  e. any multiples of 10
2a. 2 (is prime), 2×3, 3×3
  b. (cross out one 2 and one 3) $2 \times 3 \times 3 = 18$
  c. $18 \div 2 = 9$, $18 \div 6 = 3$, $18 \div 9 = 2$
  d. no, 18

Note: This mystery requires some familiarity with prime numbers and factors. In section 1 it should be clear to children that 10 is the smallest multiple of 2, 5, and 10: even though the separate divisors are 2, 5, and 2 × 5, the 2 and 5 do not have to multiplied twice. In section 2, however, children may need some help to see that 2, 2 × 3, and 3 × 3 are all contained in 2 × 3 × 3.

25. 'Rithmetic Riddles

1. 81
2. third-and-third-and-third (Other suggestions may be acceptable.)
3. **7 × 11 = 77**
4. The distance is the same, so the two spiders arrived together.
5. any group of 7, such as a week, Snow White's dwarfs, colors of a rainbow
6. three (as shown, or counterclockwise)

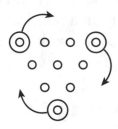

7. No; it uses a very precise figure for a very rough estimate. 5 kilometers would be fine
8. 124816 (If you start with any digit other than 1, the result will be more than six digits.)
9. The two sides of the lot (60 feet and 40 feet) add up to less than the third side (110 feet), so they cannot make a triangle.

10. 2 seconds; since the timing of each other child's beat is an exact fraction of "yours," they and you will come together every time you beat your drum.

Seconds	0	1	2
you	●		●
Hannah	●	●	●
Joe	●	●	●	●
Lila	●	●	● ●	●
Ed	●	●	● ●	● ●

Note: In Number 6, an astute child may notice that the given answer slightly increases the distance between the pins and the bowler. If so, you might have children discuss whether this is an important difference.

With Number 9, you might cut a piece of thin cardboard into strips that measure 4, 6, and 11 inches long and ask children if they can arrange the strips in a triangle.

In Number 10, you might consider a practical exercise in rhythm. Divide the class into groups and have them take turns tapping pencils while you conduct the basic beat. The faster beats could be simplified to multiples of 2.